THE INSURANCE GUIDE

-

EFFECTIVE SUCCESS TIPS AND STRATEGIES FOR INSURANCE AGENTS

Copyright © 2019 – All Rights Reserved

This book is copyright protected, and is intended for personal use only.

No parts of this publication may be reproduced in any form or by any means, including printing, scanning, photocopying, or otherwise unless explicitly stated. Any attempts to amend, sell, distribute, paraphrase, or quote the contents of this book, without the consent of the author or copyright owner can and will result in legal action.

Please note that the details included within this book are for informational purposes only. The publisher and author have made every effort to ensure the accuracy of the information contained within this book. However, they make no warranties as to the completeness of the contents herein, and hence hereby declaim any liability for errors, omissions, or contrary interpretation of the subject matter.

The information contained cannot be considered a substitute for treatment as prescribed by a therapist or other professional. By reading this book, you are assuming all risks associated with using the advice, data, and suggestions given below, with a full understanding that you, solely, are responsible for anything that may occur as a result of putting this information into action in any way – regardless of your interpretation of the advice.

TABLE OF CONTENTS

CHAPTER ONE PERSPECTIVE 5

CHAPTER TWO KNOWLEDGE 11

CHAPTER THREE EXECUTION 19

CHAPTER FOUR TEAM 24

CHAPTER FIVE MARKETING 29

CHAPTER SIX SYSTEMS 36

CHAPTER SEVEN LEADERSHIP 41

CHAPTER EIGHT CAPACITY 50

CHAPTER NINE CULTURE 54

CHAPTER TEN ENVIRONMENT 60

CHAPTER ELEVEN MODERNIZATION 65

CHAPTER TWELVE DISCIPLINE 71

CHAPTER THIRTEEN TRAINING 76

CHAPTER ONE

PERSPECTIVE

In life, it's always vital to have the right attitude in both your personal and professional life. It's quite easy to lose track of the important things during one's professional journeys. You can view your present situation while pursuing your goals and either see it as heaven or hell; it's all a matter of perspective.

Selling insurance isn't the same as marketing other physical items; it's entirely different. It's one of the most expensive things to sell to people, especially since they can't see, touch, or hold it. As an insurance agent, you're selling ideas, promises, and even trust; which make things a bit tricky if you don't have the right perspective.

You're selling yourself to the client. You need to know how to package your ideas and present them accurately. A lot of insurance agents can't handle the task and end up quitting in their first two years of working in the field.

What works for you might not work for another individual. It all comes down to how you view yourself. Having the right perspective will not only make you and your clients happy, but it will also make you feel satisfied. You can decide to recognize multiple realities by merely choosing to change your focus.

In every business venture, success or failure is all about perspective. Sometimes, short-term failures could be hidden within long-term successes, while easy wins could lead to potential losses.

You'd never make it to the big leagues in the world of insurance marketing if you run at the first sign of trouble. You might not recognize an opportunity before you if you dwell on one bad loss or disappointment. Mistakes happen, but the best thing you can do is figure out how to turn it around into something positive.

You might be finding it difficult to succeed as an insurance agent, and often wonder how people make it in the business. I'm here to tell you that it's possible. You just need the right amount of knowledge, perception, and how to properly execute each venture.

The right perspective can turn what seemed like an apparent failure or disaster into a glowing success story. It can also do the opposite as well; the key here is to figure out which way works best.

Having the right outlook in your professional life is obviously crucial to accomplishing lots of things and making significant decisions. If you're wondering how you're supposed to gain and maintain the right perspective to make sure your choices are the right ones, then there are several analogies to use.

Let's compare growing your professional life to completing a marathon. The race is quite grueling for pretty much everyone that embarks on it, but a reasonable amount still manages to finish it. And each person completes it the same way – one step at a time.

It doesn't matter what pace they start or finish with; all that counts is that they eventually finish the race they started.

Marathons and businesses can be similar in terms that it's not how fast. It's not a sprint where every step and second counts. As long as you're committed to your goals and are ready to handle every obstacle that you encounter, then you'll push through until you get to that finish line.

One of the primary reasons some insurance agents are successful while others struggle mostly has to do with their habits. The little routines, philosophies, and methodologies, are what dictate their daily activities and make them highly effective at what they do.

Sticking with a routine or habit for each week can be considered a success on its own. It's also essential to observe the practices of other insurance agents. Try surrounding yourself with other successful agents as much as possible. Most times when you're surrounded by people that are headed in the same direction as you are, it makes the process of getting to the end all the more easier.

You'll become better at your job when you associate with better insurance agents. According to Bestselling author Jim Rohn, "You're the average of the five people you spend the most time with."

Highly effective insurance agents have a sense of urgency about them. They know when to act and when to wait the market out. Failure isn't something to dread and avoid; it's part of the process. Failure means that you're on your way to success; that's if you use it as an opportunity to be better.

Most insurance agents are trained to be averse to risks, but that doesn't mean we should stop taking calculated ones in our businesses. Failure, when used in the right way, can teach us how to succeed. You never know when you'll stumble on an idea that could lead you to the next level. Regardless of how many times you fail, you have to stay committed to achieving your goals to become an effective insurance agent.

If things don't go according to the way you planned it, you just have to take a step back and figure out how to handle the situation with a fresh perspective. The secret to success is usually in the numbers – regardless of if it's good or bad since they always have something to teach us.

It takes dedication, organization, and careful planning to become a highly successful agent.

CHAPTER TWO

KNOWLEDGE

Knowledge they say is power. There are several things every insurance agent should know. One of the best ways to be effective at sales is to know your stuff because there's nothing worse than getting caught in a situation where you don't have any idea how to fix it.

No one is born with sales skills. It's something you learn and cultivate along the way. It takes time and dedication to master something before becoming a professional. Selling insurance never ends. Regardless of whatever it is you're selling. You just need to keep cultivating your skills until you don't even have to think about what you're doing; everything would come naturally to you.

A salesperson must have extensive knowledge of whatever they're selling. And that's why insurance agents need to take the time to improve their knowledge base with new and essential facts.

The significant difference between average insurance agents and the successful ones can be traced back to the early years in their careers. It doesn't matter how they got into the industry, or how many people they know. What counts is how open they were to learning new tricks, riding out the inevitable lows that come up sometimes, and adapting to the situation.

Some insurance agents adopt a myopic view and only focus on their next commission check instead of taking the time to develop skills that'll eventually set them apart from everyone else in the industry.

While it's essential to have a thorough understanding of the policy details and other technical insurance knowledge, it takes a lot more to thrive in the competitive world of insurance.

Developing Sales Skills

A sales skill is something you learn each time you carry out a job. It's developed through intentional effort. The most valuable asset an insurance agent can have is his/her ability to sell anything, especially when it seems like it'll be impossible to do.

Sales don't end in a day. Whether you're selling yourself, policies, or prospects on your agency – you're always selling something. The quicker you establish your ability to build relationships and steadily turn them into sales, the faster your career will thrive.

It might seem easier said than done, but it still happens. All you need is the right set of skills and the motivation to get started. Developing a sales skill is something you do intentionally. You need to make a conscious effort to become better through a combination of formal education, mentorship, and trial and error.

If you're still learning the ropes, try to find a way to attach yourself to someone that's already established in the business; it'll make the process a lot easier.

Your tone, pace, and the way you address people are being judged. Your prospects will probably be asking themselves if you know what you're talking about in the first place; which is why you must always act confident, even if you don't feel it.

In the end, even with digital marketing and automation allowing the agencies to capture the attention of a wider audience, it still comes down to how well you can close.

Time management is an essential skill to cultivate. Your success is mostly determined by how much you can achieve every day. A lot of individuals spend decades trying to figure out how to handle their time. The best insurance agents develop their time management skills quite early in their careers because they know how useful it will be to them as they progress.

The tough part of the time management issue is that no solution solves every individual problem. Everyone has a particular strategy that works for them and how they operate. You just have to work out the technique that fits your work plan and schedule.

Essential Knowledge Insurance Sales Agents Need

Sales and Marketing

Since most of what an insurance agent does is sell things to people, it's vital that they know the basics required in this field. You need to have the knowledge of principles and methods for showing, selling, and promoting products and services. And some of them should include; sales techniques, product demonstration, marketing strategies and tactics, and sales control systems.

The Use of English Language

Since English is the general language used by everyone in to communicate (except in countries with other languages), you'd need to have a good command of the dialect. Knowledge of the content and structure of the language includes knowing the meaning and spelling of words, composition rules, and grammar.

The ability to understand written sentences and paragraphs in work documents is highly required. Being able to communicate effortlessly with prospects sets a successful agent from mediocre ones.

Customer and Personal Service

Good insurance agents must possess the knowledge of principles and processes for providing customer and personal services. It includes; meeting quality standards for services, customer needs assessment, evaluation of customer satisfaction, and doing everything possible to meet up with the clients' needs.

Clerical Knowledge

The knowledge of administrative and accounting procedures and systems such as word processing, form designing, stenography and transcription, managing files and records, and other office procedures is also required.

Economics and Accounting

It's also essential to be well versed in economic and accounting principles and practices, the financial markets, banking, and the analysis and reporting of financial data.

Administration and Management

Insurance agents need to have the knowledge of business and management principles involved in strategic planning, allocation of resource, leadership techniques, and coordination of individuals and resources.

Law and Government

This part is especially necessary when handling sensitive cases. The knowledge of laws, legal codes, government regulations, agency rules, executive orders, court procedures and precedents is required to ease the process for insurance agents.

Communications and Media

Knowing how to use the media (especially social media platforms) to your advantage could make your entire career as an insurance agent relatively easy to navigate. While the media has its pros and cons, if you know how to utilize it, your job could get so much easier. Stock up on knowledge of media production, dissemination techniques and methods.

CHAPTER THREE

EXECUTION

In insurance, execution means the completion of a 'buy or sell' order for security. The process is pretty much similar in the various industries that have to do with sales. There's an almost consistent structure that's present in every strong and growing sales team.

Documenting the process

It involves outlining the sales process and tracking every step you make with your client. When you note every single action taken during a job, it makes it easier to go back and retrace your steps if anything goes wrong during the process.

Steps to help with Execution

1. **Develop and Implement a Strategy**

Before you embark on any process, the first move you should make is to lay out specific plans to reach your target prospects – both old clients and new ones. If it helps, sometimes it's good to practice with targets first before going out into the wild (figuratively of course).

2. Identify your Prospects

When you and your team (if you're part of one) figure out the particular type of people you're going to be selling to; you'd have achieved one of the most critical steps in implementing the sales plan.

3. Create a Sales Pipeline

This tactic will help you figure out the demand for your service. It paves the way for customer satisfaction and an increase in client base.

4. Integrate Marketing and Sales Programs

It takes excellent marketing strategies to make prospects aware of what you offer and then turning them into paying customers. With the right team working with you, your sales plan can be brought to life.

5. Measure your Strategies, and Adjust if Necessary

While creating your plans and strategies, it's essential to take into consideration external factors that could affect the process. The key here is to measure and adjust it when the need arises. Just changing things for the sake of change doesn't always work; but when it's essential, change can create a whole new level of productivity and success.

6. Drive the Deals through the Pipeline

While your team pushes deals through to its completion, it's your job to see its ability to drive profits upward.

7. Carry out Progress Reviews at Regular Intervals

While it's essential to make progress on any task, it's vital to check if you're on the right track regularly; because it's better to stop halfway when you notice something isn't working out, rather than seeing the mistakes at the end. Progress reviews help you figure out what's working and what isn't, so you can fix the issue before it's too late.

8. Deliver Results

With every task you perform, it all boils down to the results you deliver at the end. You need to focus on the things that would make this process all the more easier for you.

Common Issues that Affects Execution

- Failure to fully document the sales process or update it. This mistake often leads to the agents making their process that cannot be easily measured, tracked, or optimized.

- Focusing more on completing tasks rather than meeting performance metrics.
- Inadequate training of the agents
- Not measuring the execution plan for its effectiveness which often leads to kinks developing along the line with no easy fix.

CHAPTER FOUR

TEAM

Sometimes it's easy to get lost in the chaos of trying to manage your team; which causes individuals to get stressed and ultimately result in everyone having a bad day.

Working together as a team not only reduces your workload and increase your speed – which benefits your customers, but it also minimizes your stress levels and fosters a great working environment.

Working as a team helps you and your teammates work better together especially after figuring out how to use each other's strengths to complete the task a lot faster.

One of the biggest issues with insurance teams is that they require more motivation than regular teams because of the nature of the job. It's quite easy to get frustrated if things aren't going so well; that's why the team leader's role is vital.

They have to come up with unique ways to motivate and keep the team focused on each task, especially the tedious ones.

If you happen to be a team leader, here are a few things to consider;

- **Recruiting**

It's one of the most important functions of the team leader – recruiting new agents. Due to the nature of the job (mostly working on commissions) it's not for everyone, that's why it takes a special kind of patience to convince people to join. The team leader must keep searching for new talent everywhere he/she finds him/herself. They'd meet individuals with varying backgrounds and have to evaluate their chances for success.

- **Training**

Most times the agents you might end up hiring might come from different walks of life and have very little in common (except working in insurance). It's now up to you as the leader to bring everyone together and find common ground for everyone to relate with. It takes more than being able to meet and talk to people easily to make a good salesperson. Your teammates must have a sound knowledge of what their selling and to whom. They must know the techniques involved in prospecting new clients and convincing them that they need financial security. Your primary role as an insurance team leader is to hone these skills in your agents.

- **Case Assistance**

As it's to be expected, your team members will definitely run into situations where they need your help. It's essential that you make the time to assist them when necessary. You need to take the time to review sales files with each member and provide guidance on sales opportunity given a particular prospects personal and financial information. Then go on a sales call with him/her and review their techniques. This process will allow you to coach the agents so that they'd learn to be more productive on their own.

- **Value Everyone**

One of the best ways to create a great team is by building an environment of value. Everyone on your team has a fresh insight and a point of view to contribute. You just need to make sure that they're given the opportunity. Avoid downplaying the response to their opinions on strategies and goals.

- **Monitor Sales Results**

One of the few ways to measure success is through the sales results. It's why you need to monitor them to identify positive or negative trends continually. Analyzing the results for clues will help you figure out if your training efforts are valid or not. It's also through this that you'd be able to decide which team members met their quotas, the ones that need special attention, and the ones that need to be fired.

The role of the team leader requires a lot of tact and patience, and also a certain amount of ruthlessness concerning the bottom line.

The following are traits of good team members;

- Dedication
- Entrepreneurial spirit
- A good understanding of the insurance world
- High energy
- Great communication skills
- High commitment and investment levels
- Being able to be coached
- Possessing the sense of urgency
- Highly organized
- Getting involved in the process

CHAPTER FIVE

MARKETING

There are several insurance marketing ideas online, but very few of them will actually help you out. Most of them tend to work as one-offs, and just work to get you one or two new policyholders, but they aren't necessarily sustainable to beat out the competition.

That's mainly what marketing is about – finding a way to stand out from the rest. So that prospects will choose your insurance company from the rest, only one marketing campaign won't do the trick; you need several ones.

One of the first hurdles you're going to have to get through to attract life-long clients is to break through the online noise to reach them. And thanks to the internet, today's prospects don't like buying what they haven't adequately researched online yet. They naturally view insurance companies with suspicion;

especially when they've had unpleasant encounters in the past.

Consumers of today are used to instant, seamless, and sophisticated shopping experiences; and they expect purchasing insurance to be no different from the rest. They need the process to be as easy as buying new shoes from Amazon.

There are several strategies and ideas you can use to help with marketing insurance, and they include;

Improving your Website

In this digital age, your website is usually the first form of interaction policyholders will have with your company. If they connect with your page within ten seconds of clicking on it, they'll move on to the next provider. There are three rules that you need to keep in mind when designing your website. It should be **Fast**, **secure**, and **Mobile-Friendly**.

Research shows that over fifty percent of searches happen from mobile phones. Not everyone has instant access to a computer, but they're always with their phones. So, if you should hand out your card to a prospect, and they want to check out your site, the first thing they'd do is search for it on their phones.

It should tell you something about the customer experience and usability most customers expect. And it isn't just enough to be user-friendly; your site has to load in under three seconds.

Try to make sure your contact information is placed front and center. Most times, people's eyes tend to move towards the top right-hand corner. Include lots of calls-to-action. Install a chat feature to answer instant questions of the prospects. Use colors that will convey meanings to them because they tend to influence an individual's emotions

You could also create a blog to help generate traffic to your website and build trust. Blog posts play significant roles in consumers researching products and services.

Invest in Search Engine Optimization (SEO)

Before they can interact with your site, policyholders need to be able to find you online. Since ninety-three percent of online experiences begin with search engines, you need to find a way to situate yourself at the top of the results page. A lot of people don't bother checking out the subsequent pages.

So, you'll need to invest in SEO if you want to get your insurance company on the first page of Google or other search engines. There are over two hundred ranking factors, but here are some of the major ones;

- Your website has to be mobile-friendly
- It needs to be secured (HTTPS vs. HTTP)
- The page needs meta descriptions and optimized title tags
- Your website's content needs to be of a quality level
- Your site needs to be fast
- It needs to have optimized images and be fast

- You need lots of quality backlinks and social signals.

Make it Simple

Insurance can be quite overwhelming for people that don't understand what you're selling – especially the young ones. Don't give them too many options on your website's main pages because it could tip your visitors over the edge. Figure out the most important things that your prospects want to see, and focus on them.

You could create an interactive guide on your site to show your prospects the basics of insurance. Create short videos (less than two minutes) that'll explain the different types of insurance coverage and post them on your site and your YouTube page (those are necessary too).

Pay Attention to Online Reviews

Word of mouth has always been a thing, except now it has evolved to reach millions of people all over the world. Various platforms have spaces for their customers to drop reviews on products and services which tend to help or ruin them.

Research shows that seventy-nine percent of individuals ask friends and families for referrals whenever they want to buy insurance. Another sixty-five percent go to colleagues and social acquaintances for help. Online reviews are trusted even more than personal recommendations.

Lots of insurance agencies tend to ignore online reviews, and it ends up affecting their businesses. Whether you pay attention to it, these reviews play a significant role in how people view what you're selling. Whether they accept it or not depends mostly on what they've heard about it from others.

Try to embrace online reviews and use it to your advantage, especially since very few insurance companies use it. Create strategies to generate raving reviews by asking your policyholders to leave some. Or you could install review-generating software; there are several ones to pick from.

Embrace Video Marketing

A lot of individuals understand things like insurance better when they watch an agent explain it to them in a short video. Make use of platforms like YouTube to expand your business and reach new prospects. Create informational or how-to videos and post online. And at the end of the video, feature testimonials from policyholders you've helped. The fastest way to promote your brand is through satisfied clients.

CHAPTER SIX

SYSTEMS

A system is a procedure, method, process, or course of action that's designed to realize specific results. The parts work together for the good of the whole. Systems and processes are the crucial building blocks of most companies and firms. Every facet of your business is part of a system that can be managed and improved when you apply the right principles.

Business systems are also strategic responses to a chain of events that take place within different divisions. They could include contractual agreements, payment policies, marketing management, and customer care amongst others.

From a business point of view, the system is supposed to connect all of the organizations' intricate parts and steps to work together for the achievement of an efficient strategy. Applying defined ideologies and practices to the systems and processes which deliver value to the customers end up creating what's known as business systems.

Creating effective ones often unifies the decision-making and problem-solving aspects of the organization. Most common tools for this process are usually taught and expected to be utilized at various levels. Business systems tend to cover how we lead our clients and connect them to operational strategies.

Having an effective business system is the only practical way to manage the crucial details of your operation. It could be as simple as creating a checklist within an hour or two or engaging more complex systems that take weeks to implement.

The best systems often consider elements like components, design, individual, speed, quality, and measurement. The best systems tend to take things like waste and inefficiency out of your business and help you provide what your clients want every single time. They solve the problem of weak sales growth, customer dissatisfaction, low-profit margins, poor performance, excessive costs, employee turnover, and inadequate cash flow among other things.

The best companies are the ones that have the best business systems and processes. A lot of highly successful companies in this era started with one major innovative system (McDonald's, Google, Federal Express overnight delivery to name a few). These companies and thousand others like them built fortunes on one or more notable systems that serve customers better than any other industries within their target market.

Identify what your business system is and elevate them to higher performance and enjoy the profits along the way. Find ways to build networks within each business function, allowing the systems to run the business, while the individuals run the systems.

Reasons to Implement a Business System

- **To Improve Performance**

Part of this category involves implementing strategic planning, business processes, and strategy creation throughout the organization. A business system takes care of the agency's future and ensures that you meet up with the client's expectations and improve the brand; since they're the key to developing a healthy business. Using a systematic approach will allow you to have constant information on areas that need improvement, and ensure that you're at the top of your game.

- **To Meet Client's Expectations**

When you use a systematic approach, you'll be able to analyze, measure, compare and test every possibility of what your customers want and don't need. It'll provide you with constant information on areas of your pitch that needs improvement, and you'll also be attuned with the needs of your clients.

- **To Get Consistent Results**

Regardless of the area you're focusing on (safety or quality) a business system is designed to produce efficient, effective, and repeatable results. The system is there to fix your processes.

- **To Reduce Cost and Increase Profit**

A sound business system is there to reduce costs without taking any shortcuts that could lead to the erosion of profits and quality.

CHAPTER SEVEN

LEADERSHIP

When lots of people think about who a leader is, they tend to think of influential people in the world who push ideas forward. That isn't necessarily who a leader is – it could be anyone. Your ideal could be getting in the way of discovering and cultivating true leaders at your insurance agency.

Before going any further, the first thing you need to know is that leadership wears many hats. The leadership style you need could change depending on the situation at hand. It could be as diverse as your employees or team members. While in some cases your firm might need a charismatic leader to move ideas forward, in other instances they could require an empathetic one to help create calm and work through conflicts in the business.

There are several definitions of what leadership entails just as there are many of them. Just as every individual is different from others around them, so also are leaders different. Everyone has what they're good at and how to utilize it to the full advantage.

Some people might be content to follow a leader with street smarts while others would prefer someone who's been trained to focus on the big picture. It's not easy to unlock the secrets of effective leadership, because there's a lot to it than meets the eye.

Most of what leadership boils down to are effective communication that;

- Relates a plan of action that advances the point of view
- And unites a group behind a particular point of view

For leadership to be truly effective, the individuals behind the leaders must internalize the leader's plan of action and point of view so that it'll guide their behavior even when he/she isn't around to observe them. Leadership consists of creating a self-sustaining culture of actions and thoughts that are consistent with the stated purpose of the team.

If you're in the position to appoint someone to take charge of an account or team, you need to consider their potentials first. You have to consider individuals that can adapt and grow into increasingly complex roles and environments.

When you're tasked with filling or creating new insurance jobs at your agency, try to look beyond an individual's experience and make use of leadership potentials as filters. Try searching for people that are passionate about the job and not just competent enough. Note the ones with a combination of ambition and humility.

How to Bring Forward New Insurance Leaders

- Look out for the ones that bring ideas to life and like to catalyze new projects.

- Give him/her a trial run where they are given an opportunity to lead, and see how they respond to it.
- Encourage them to evaluate their successes and failures. Watch how they handle the setbacks. Good leaders aren't afraid to hold themselves responsible for the failure of the team.
- Place the individual under challenging situations, then observe and support (if necessary) them as they make their way through these challenges. The circumstances could involve anything from, hard decisions about priorities, sophisticated communications, and multitasking.
- Always find the opportunity to coach and mentor your emerging leaders to help them through the trials of leadership.

Since no one is born a leader, we all have to work hard to hone our skills whenever we find ourselves in situations that require our abilities. Just as with every industry, insurance has been influenced by both negative and positive leadership over the years. In today's economy that's filled with changing technology and younger workforce, strong leadership is especially important right now.

Leadership Principles to Observe

Understanding and applying these four principles in your daily life and business will allow you to become a stronger leader, grow your agency, and gain influence with the people around you.

1. You're only as effective as your leadership abilities

There isn't any part of your organization that leadership won't affect. Your ability to lead effectively determines your efficacy. You don't need to spend all your time thinking of new ideas or processes to implement. What you desperately need is improved leadership abilities.

There are countless reasons why the insurance industry lacks positive leaders, but the bottom line is that great leadership requires daily hard work. It doesn't just happen overnight while you're sleeping. There's no magic potion to create great leaders; it's something that has to be developed intentionally and gradually.

2. It's more than just a title

Leadership is mostly about influence, and it's not the title that gives it to you. In some cases, leadership and management are lumped together as if they're the same thing; but that's not the case. While both of them are essential in an organization, they're very different skills. While leadership is about influencing the people around you, management has to do with maintaining systems and processes. And the best way to know if you have the influence is indicated through your followers.

3. You're your greatest leadership challenge

Before you can be equipped to lead anyone, you must first be able to lead yourself; which is why self-leadership is the highest calling of control. When you've been able to grow yourself effectively, you'll then be able to do the same for the people around you. And one of the great things about self-leadership is that it's a never-ending process. One of the significant characteristics a leader should have is becoming a lifelong learner. Regardless of how much you think you already know, there's still more knowledge to be gained in the industry, and room to grow. Influential leaders understand that leadership is not an event but a continuous process. While self-leadership isn't easy, in the end, it's gratifying.

4. Leadership is about adding value to everyone around you

Most times during the process of leading a group of people, leaders often get caught up in the details and miss the whole point of the situation. They forget the most crucial purpose of leadership which is adding value to the lives of those they serve. If you're unsure of whether you're adding value to people's lives or not, just ask your followers if you're making things better for them or not.

Most times the insurance industry tends to throw around the word "Value-added" when referring to their products or services. But when the client or business you're trying to add value to their lives doesn't feel valued, there's very little you can add to make an impact on the situation. To add value to people's lives, you must first appreciate them. It's not always easy since effective leadership takes effort.

Adding value is about listening to the needs of the people around you. It's pretty much impossible to lead anyone if you don't know the first thing about them or haven't listened to what they have to say to understand how to serve them best.

Effective leaders listen, and learn, before leading the people around them.

CHAPTER EIGHT

CAPACITY

According to the International Risk Management Institute (IRMI), Capacity is the most substantial amount of insurance that a company or market is capable of writing. It also refers to how much more business a firm or market can write based on the amount of surplus capital that's available. The financial strength of an agency determines capacity and as a result, affects the price and availability of renters insurance.

Underwriting Capacity

This represents an insurer's ability to retain risk. Ordinarily, an insurance company's potential for profitability depends on how much risk it's willing to take. The more risks it accepts by underwriting new insurance policies, the more premiums it amasses and later invests.

The underwriting capacity of a company is a very crucial component of its operations. The capacity can change over time based on how the factors used to calculate its capacity change.

In some cases, insurance companies can increase their underwriting capacity by endorsing policies that cover less volatile risks. Take, for instance, a company could refuse to write new property insurance coverage areas that are prone to hurricanes, but still, cover hazards from theft and fire. Reducing the risks of policies written decreases the possibility that the company will have to pay out claims.

As with reinsurance treaties, insurers are also capable of increasing their underwriting capacity by relinquishing their obligations to a third party. In a reinsurance contract, the individual assumes some of the insurer's liability in exchange for a portion of the premiums or a fee paid by the policyholder.

The insurer can underwrite a new policy when the liabilities assumed by the reinsurer no longer counts against the underwriting capacity of the conceding company. This doesn't necessarily mean that the insurer can abandon the obligations it cedes in the reinsurance contract. If a claim should occur, the ceding company is still responsible.

In situations where the insurer goes bankrupt, the ceding insurer has to pay for claims made against its original underwritten policies. That's why it's vital for the insurer to know the financial health of the reinsurer, including the total amount of risks they've agreed to handle through other reinsurance contracts.

Life Insurance Capacity Calculators

LIC Calculators estimate insurance capacity by applying the companies' financial underwriting guidelines to the info provided by the clients. It then subtracts the number of life insurance coverage currently in force to evaluate how much of the full capacity could be potentially purchased.

The tool helps minimize financial underwriting problems and increases life insurance sales.

CHAPTER NINE

CULTURE

According to Ned Morse, co-author of "Switch Points: Culture Change on the Fast Track to Business Success," culture can be defined as the patterns of behaviors that are discouraged or encouraged by individuals and systems over a period. It's also about behavior that's tolerated by people, leaders, and systems over time.

When your vision resonates with policyholders and clients, and empower, motivate, and inspire the staff, it'll ultimately determine the supporting culture.

Every cultural change should support your vision, and ultimately improve the experience of customers and stakeholders and support your business. In anything you do, try to ask yourself how any cultural change you wish to achieve would be felt by your clients in their interactions with your company and its people.

Culture has the power to influence staffing and retention; which makes sense since a poor culture could drag down employee sentiment and productivity. When a lot of organizations hear the word, they equate it to going crazy. It's true that a lot of cultures are more bizarre than several others; you just need to create on that suits your workforce and brand. You don't need to go about trying to replicate other company's own, come up with a culture that best fits your firm's unique characteristics.

An organization's culture is usually the heart of the company, and strong ones keep your personnel engaged and working to their full potential.

Culture, Values, and Behaviors

Most times in business, it all comes down to these three characteristics. While they might be seen as 'soft,' they're actually the things that drive the business forward or place it at risk. Experts believe it all comes down to who you are and what you care about (Values), the shared conventions that guide what you do and how it's done (Culture), and what you actually say or do (Behavior).

Culture as the differentiator is the key to realizing a company's potential. It could be your biggest ally or greatest enemy; it all depends on how you handle the situation. Lots of insurers are trying to remodel their culture, but a lot of them are still failing to translate their high-level intentions into actual changes in ways their people behave or make decisions during the instants that matter the most.

It takes more than communication and training alone to drive change. Culture cuts across all the major competitive differentiators for insurers as they seek to create an environment that inspires employees to accept innovation wholeheartedly and engage with clients more closely.

The right culture can now be considered as the key to engaging with clients and responding to their rapidly changing expectations while making sure that the decision-making process reflects the values of the company in the moments that matter the most.

The right culture also fosters innovation, quick decision-making, and the willingness to embrace new ideas. A strong and effective culture is a lot highly connected with sustainable high performance than with strategy, product coverage, or operating model.

Cultures will always differ, but that that doesn't make one superior to the other; although they have common foundations. They include;

- A clear and a convincing sense of purpose which attracts talent and guides expectations
- Engaging employees
- Creativity, curiosity, and a readiness to challenge
- Alignment
- Making long-term decisions that have impacts which include outcomes for customers, stakeholders, and colleagues.

You don't necessarily require a new digital strategy to get ahead. What you need is a business model and culture that places the customer at its core, and seamlessly facilitated by technology.

Cultural change isn't an end in itself; instead, its overriding objective is to improve the performance of your business.

Rules for Changing Culture in an Organization

i. Ensure that your vision, purpose, and values are clear, concrete, and actionable.
ii. Align leaders to this vision and encourage them to lead the change. The actions of leaders set the tone for their followers.
iii. Involve the entire organization and insert change through moments that matter. Since it isn't possible to change a whole culture overnight, the key behaviors can be shifted in a relatively short

time frame. Engaging everyone is essential to the success of the organization.

iv. Measure progress and behavior. It's almost impossible to measure culture, so behavior will have to do since it's the tangible manifestation of culture. The measurement can provide a great reflection of the overall culture of a company.

v. Make use of the change levers to reinforce behavioral change.

Your culture should create excitement about winning in the market and not the fear of losing. Take time to understand every factor involved in this process and design your working environment according; which brings us to the next topic.

CHAPTER TEN

ENVIRONMENT

When it comes to environmental change or uncertainties, insurance companies have been in the forefront dealing with the issues. Extreme weather event poses great risks to property insurers as well as health and life insurance providers. The success of the insurance industry depends mostly on successfully anticipating and handling the risks.

When it comes to the environment and its ever-changing dynamics, insurance companies are always concerned with the way things play out. They rely on statistics and probabilities to price products based on past loss. And now with the environment and climate changing every day, the statistics aren't entirely reliable predictors.

Environmental changes bring about doubt and ambiguity into the once historical pricing process since the past events aren't an entirely reliable predictor of future events. Insurers became dependent on catastrophe modelers that assess an insurer's possible maximum loss to provide pricing guidance. Because of global warming and insufficient data due to prior events, the predictive accuracy of these models hasn't proven as great as they once had.

Even though most environmental change is way beyond our immediate control, several costs of the changes can be avoided by taking action as soon as possible (Mitigation). Several Insurance companies have taken steps to ease future Environmental impacts by lessening greenhouse gas emissions. Insurance could also be a valuable tool in adaptation processes towards global environmental change.

The role of insurance is to bring a little bit of predictability, manageability, and stability in an otherwise chaotic world. There are three direct impacts that environmental changes can impose on insurance. They include;

- Increasing premium rates

- A lack of insurance available for individuals living in risky geographical zones from the private sector
- Using higher deductibles to shift additional risks to policyholders.

Insurance availability depends on two factors;

- The insurance company's ability to finance the risk associated with the insured
- And the expectation that the underwritten insurance would be profitable.

Consequently, if the premium is set high in consideration of the environmental consequences, individuals might be reluctant to get insured because of the higher premium. This particular kind of tradeoff poses a great impasse for both parties involved.

In most cases, insurance companies are less likely to meet the needs of locations that are prone to disasters (areas susceptible to earthquakes or tsunamis).

Environmental Change serves as a new Business Opportunities

From the point-of-view of investors, the new changes that the environment is undergoing tend to represent potential business opportunities for the insurance industry. Just like any commercial enterprise, insurance agencies want to gain new business and improve market shares.

And as a result, several of them are designing and building new and innovative products that'll stand the test of time. The business also needs to understand its customers entirely if it's going to manage risks and increase revenue profitability.

The good news about the environmental changes is that several of the solutions are within reach, and a growing number of insurers are 'thinking green' when developing their new insurance products and services.

Some of the solutions to global warming are not only achievable but are also economically and socially beneficial. Insurance companies can use their economic potential for the justification of greenhouse gas emissions over the following decades.

CHAPTER ELEVEN

MODERNIZATION

As with every form of business in this modern day, embracing the digital age is essential for organizations that don't want to be left behind. The journey to digital insurance involves a significant amount of technological transformation.

Several insurance companies are well into their efforts to modernize things, and most of it focuses on core administration systems, that address the portfolio of older policy systems that have accumulated over time.

The task of modernization isn't something to be trivialized. For example, a typical midsize to large insurer in the U.S. maintains around four or more policy administration systems, and several of them have ten or more portfolios. The costs and complexity of managing these multiple – redundant systems can be overwhelming most times and often distract a carrier from newly critical tasks.

Insurers must invest in next-generation analytics and new customer-centric distribution to avoid being marginalized. The challenge now is for them to tackle the legacy while building the new simultaneously.

Regardless of what most software vendors tell their clients, there's no silver bullet for modernization. No off-the-shelf policy-administration software system will solve the challenges that you'll face during the process. Avoid implementing an entirely new policy administration platform, as this often costs tens of millions of dollars; which end up being for nothing.

Depending on the admin system and its function in the organization, sometimes it's better to do nothing. Leave the system in place and focus instead on reducing maintenance costs.

Embracing Mobility and Social Media

It's almost impossible to interact with any firm or agency without being redirected to their website,

Facebook page, Twitter Feed, or any other social media platform.

Over the past decades, most insurance companies have witnessed a 180-degree turn in the manner at which they're expected to interact with clients; whether they're the end consumer or distribution channel.

Previously it was the insurer that dictated how the clients interacted with them (either through call centers, direct mail, or offices), now it's the other way around thanks to social media.

A mobility strategy is a significant requirement in today's market. Enjoying a standard view from multiple devices and providing vital information across various channels is now becoming the new normal.

In a world that's evolving digitally every day, it's a challenge for insurers to stay current; and the ones that manage to remain available and easily accessible through the channels of today will gain the most market shares.

The look, feel, and branding should always remain clear and consistent. The prospects need to be able to tell from a glance that they're looking at the same company to build trust and loyalty. Even if you're going to make significant changes, try and keep it as close to the original brand as possible to prevent confusion.

The Possibility of Upgrading your System Instead of replacing it completely

For some companies that support vendor applications, upgrading to the latest version is an excellent strategy for modernization. Sadly, lots of insurance companies wait too long to take advantage of the program. Over the years, several vendor applications have come and gone, leaving the insurers with unsupported applications and no particular migration paths to new systems. So, instead of what should have just been routine upgrades, they're left to face major licensing decisions and complete replacement of the system.

There's a Great Chance that System Replacement might only Solve Part of your Issues

This step is the most commonly recommended by outside vendors, but insurers rarely listen to all the facts about the potential costs and the effect on the environment.

In cases that involve policy administration systems, a replacement system might be implemented for only new products, and the older one outsourced or retained.

If there's no credible vendor package available, system replacement and consolidation may not be practical. The same can also be said if the functional gap between the systems is too high, or if the cost of replacement is too much for the company's size.

CHAPTER TWELVE

DISCIPLINE

Market discipline in this context can be said to be the ability of investors, customers, intermediaries (agents), and evaluators (analysts, auditors) to influence and monitor the management of insurance companies. Here the clients assess the financial strength and service quality of the insurers.

Theoretically, customers and investors have a direct influence on management decisions, while intermediaries and investors have both direct and indirect impact on it. Take, for example, a situation where customers or investors react to the market signals set by changes in ratings, which is directly influenced by customers and indirectly influenced by evaluators.

Since the indirect influence of the evaluators can lead to a direct one by customers and investors, they might also have the opportunity to exert a direct influence, assuming the managers are keen to do anything possible to prevent reduced ratings.

Another method of measuring market discipline is to look at it as customer-driven. And as a result, the studies on the insurance discipline consider premium growth and lapse. Just as with everything else, there are limitations in measuring customer-driven market discipline. Here, premiums are not the price of insurance; instead, it's the price multiplied by the quantity.

It isn't necessarily easy to observe insurance prices – and even if the information were available, it would be quite difficult to compare insurers since the fundamental expectations of claims costs used to estimate rates might be different and not observable.

In the area of insurance, market discipline focuses on the sensitivity of risk of customer demand, and the willingness of investors to pay for equity and debt. Before measuring market discipline, we need first to identify market signals that affect the risk sensitivity of investors/customers. And after that, evaluate whether the signal has a substantial impact on our measures of market discipline.

Market discipline is relevant to regulatory issues, as it's usually the third fundamental pillar. It's expected that a transparent market will require less obvious interventions by regulators as the participants force appropriate firm behavior. It depends on the strength of the influence of market discipline for it to be relied on for successful regulation.

It's not entirely possible for market discipline to completely replace regulation. It could be argued that policyholders with excellent information should be free to buy insurance with a lower safety level in a perfect and arbitrage-free market, as long as the contract pricing is fair.

In this world, the fully informed policyholder could choose to accept the default risk, and as a result, there won't be any need for capital regulation.

The most important impediments to market discipline in insurance include;

- The complexity of financial products
- The judgment-proof problem that occurs in cases of compulsory insurance impedes market discipline
- Indirect or implicit market distortions
- An increase in financial leverage which also increases the company's risk

In this context, we should also expect more market discipline in reinsurance than with insurance since the first one only covers commercial business while the second covers both personal and commercial lines. One implication for policymakers is that when equating personal and commercial insurance, it reveals that the market discipline is weak in some areas and strong in others.

Market discipline focuses on the risk sensitivity of customer demand for insurance products and on investor willingness to pay for equity and debt. An indication from the banking sector reveals that market discipline can work quite effectively. However, there are some aspects where the banking area is different from the insurance sector, so not all the findings gotten from banking could be generalized to the insurance industry.

CHAPTER THIRTEEN

TRAINING

Training new (especially the younger generation) insurance agents isn't always a walk in the park. It requires a certain kind of commitment and patience. If you find yourself in the position of teaching these recruits, you just have to remember what it was like when you were in their shoes. Someone (probably) took the time to show you most of what you know today, so now's the time to give back to the community.

It's understandable for new insurance agents to feel overwhelmed as they begin navigating the complex world of sales, insurance, customer service, and even management of the agency.

Stop focusing on how hard it was for you as a trainee

Most times veteran agents spend most of their time telling everyone how hard it was for them while starting, and how they had to figure out pretty much everything on their own. In some cases, this might be true, but that doesn't mean the recruits have to go through the same difficulties you suffered if you can help them.

The truth is that the more you support these newbies, the more money they'll make for you. Pushing new employees to figure out the job on their own often causes lots of turnovers.

Performing random prospect spot-checks is vital

Randomly select prospects they've been working on and make them explain all they can about their process for making contact, identifying the client's needs, closing the sale, and showing the value of the agency. You basically grill them on every aspect of the project and how they handled it to see how fast they're learning or adjusting to the team.

Random checks allow you to track the progress of your trainees and offer up opportunities to correct their mistakes.

Force your recruits to practice sales regularly

The thing with practicing sales ability is that almost everybody hates doing it even though they know it'll help them get better. And as a result, your new agents would probably try to avoid doing it as much as possible. It's your job to continue nudging them every chance you get to practice.

New salespeople should practice selling insurance amongst themselves to help improve their skills and confidence levels.

Send them networking as regularly as possible

Sometimes it might get boring sitting behind a desk every single day; which is why you should send out your trainees every once in a while to test their marketing skills and switch their routines.

Send them to as many networking events as possible to make contacts and represent the agency. To make things interesting, you could set a specific goal for them to achieve before coming back to the office. It could be to hand out a certain number of business cards or getting a particular amount of LinkedIn connections and contact information.

Try turning sales into a game to bring out the competitive streaks in your recruits. You could set a particular prize (or perks) for the first person with the most sales or referrals or contacts. It could be anything to keep the fun spirit alive.

Always set the best example

You always have to be cautious of how you behave and act around your staff or people in general because someone might be watching your moves to learn something from you. They could be paying close attention to the things you say and do to develop their idea of what's good and bad.

You don't necessarily need to be the best salesperson in the office – that's not your job. You just have to act in the right manner since you have people looking up to you.

If you're the kind of person that talks behind the backs of clients or say bad things about the carriers you're selling for, then your trainees might end up following in your footsteps. And the chances of everything blowing up in your face would be astronomical.

Team up your trainees with veterans

Learning by assimilation is a great way to turn new insurance agents into pretty good ones especially when they're paired with the best in the game. Although, this tactic might not always work for everyone since not all great salespeople are good educators or even know how to teach others.

Allow the recruit to shadow one of your best agents for a week or more and watch them do what they do best. Encourage them to ask questions after each encounter to facilitate the learning process.

Don't be scared to give them the hardest leads

People tend to learn from their mistakes, so make sure you allow your recruits to work on sales that might be harder than their usual ones. Let learn that selling insurance isn't something they can half-ass. They need to put all their focus and energy on every task they're assigned, no matter how trivial it might seem to them.

Give your newbies the easiest and hardest leads, but never the best ones. Save those for when you're confident they'd do a great job with it. They can get lots of experiences without making mistakes in excellent opportunities.

Five Tips for the New Agents

1. Improve your Customer Service Skills

In insurance (and pretty much any other business) you'd have to deal with clients that expect the best customer service as quickly as possible. Since the customer is always right, you're going to have to be as accommodating as possible. Interpersonal skills are compulsory here.

In a highly competitive business like the insurance industry, customer service usually sets competitors apart from each other. Your skills might be what give your agency the edge it needs.

2. Dress for Success

Everyone knows that first impressions matter the most especially in the insurance world. You need to know how to dress for every occasion while scouting for prospects. It might seem harsh, but we tend to form a perception of an individual based on what they're wearing and how they look. Always keep your appearance clean and classy.

3. Find ways to Relate to your Clients

If you're not a great conversationalist, then you might have to learn a thing or two. Inquiring about your prospect's family and life will help jump-start the conversation and put the both of you at ease. Remember to listen more and always give your clients room to express themselves, while still dropping reasonable amounts of information about yourself to make them feel comfortable.

4. Be Transparent

Transparency during the sales process and after it is especially important. You need to work hard to build a sense of trust between you and the client. If it seems like you're hiding something from the world, then your prospects might not feel too eager to do business with you. It might make things more comfortable if you educate them on how to carry out their due diligence on you.

- **It Pays to be Persistent**

You might have all the talent in the world but might not go far in life if you're not tenacious. It's one of the essential qualities an insurance agent should have to succeed in the industry. It's true that positive and high energy can often rub off on the people around you. Persistence is one quality that you need to develop and continuously work on to prevail in the insurance business.

As with any profession, business is tough (more so in the insurance industry), and it takes time, effort, and even failure to become a master. You don't have to rush it; just take your time to enjoy the ride because it's all worth it in the end.

www.ingramcontent.com/pod-product-compliance
Lightning Source LLC
Chambersburg PA
CBHW020605220526
45463CB00006B/2456